Special Acknowledgements

I want to say thank you to the following people who inspired my program and this book.

My amazing husband Jim is an Occupational Therapist who specialized in treating autistic children with developmental delays. He knows a significant amount about how children develop and learn, as well as how they resist learning.

My sister Cherie is an elementary school teacher with extensive experience regarding children's learning. Her stories and insight have been invaluable to me.

My mother has always been a great example of a mother's unconditional love for her children. She also taught me the importance of making consequences clear in advance so that children could be responsible for their own actions.

My father taught me from a very young age, the importance of work ethic. He helped me to learn that my future was ultimately my responsibility. The first step, if I wanted to be successful, was relying on myself and not waiting for others to do things for me.

My close friends being mothers themselves, filled with stories of their own, have led to the creation of this program. Thank you to Marla, Kristen and Sheryl. I enjoyed our time as we talked in depth about the quirks of children and motherhood during our Lunch Ladies time.

My neighbors Sydney, Abby, Ramona and Jen who encouraged me to get this book written! Some of them were already implementing the system into their families, which helped encourage me to share my program with others.

Special thanks to Jim, Glenn, Meg, and Crystal for reading my manuscript and giving me constructive feedback on organization, grammar and presentation.

My children have of course been a wonderful inspiration to me. Brielle, Marissa (name changed), Connor, Jack, Haedyn and Jensen. They have all been such good sports throughout this process and have been excited to be the main "characters" in this book.

Although I am the sole developer of "Respect Rocks", I do not believe I would have been able to do it without the amazing insight that all of these wonderful people have given me.

Respect is not given, it is earned.

Respect is not innate, it is learned.

INTRODUCTION

When I created the Respect Rocks Behavior Program, I was a 34-year-old mother to six children. Brielle age fourteen, Marissa age thirteen, Connor age ten, Jack age nine, Haedyn age seven and Jensen age five. I gave birth to Connor, Haedyn and Jensen. The others I was blessed with through re-marriage.

Over the years, as a mother to six children with very different personalities, coming from multiple homes and parenting styles, I found myself continually frustrated with discipline. We were a blended family, so there were different perspectives, experiences, rules and expectations being brought into our home. It was difficult to be consistent with all of the children. Some children were with us all the time, others were there half the time and still others were only there occasionally. I was also trying to effectively teach them all to take care of themselves, each other, and our home. They were constantly disregarding what I would tell them to do. They rarely did their chores the way I asked and they almost never picked up after themselves.

More importantly, the arguing, fighting, name-calling and disrespect between them was at an all time high. It drove me crazy. I was constantly being forced to repeat myself over and over again. Whether I was telling them repeatedly to clean up after themselves or to simply be nice to each other, I felt like a broken record with absolutely no results.

Although I would like to place all of the blame on my unruly children, I would be lying if I said they were 100% at fault for my frustration. I will admit it, I am kind of a pushover and sometimes my follow through is a little lacking. Children quickly learn this and use it to their advantage. And why wouldn't they? Don't get me wrong, I have good intentions when it comes to discipline as well as teaching, training, and rearing children to become upstanding adults. Sometimes I am just too darn exhausted to follow through with the consequences.

This leads to a nasty cycle. I lay down the law...my kids follow it for a short period of time, I ask again...they ignore me...I ask again...they ignore me....I ask again...they ignore me.....I'm too tired to ask again....so I try to ignore the behavior until I can't take it anymore. Then I flip out and yell and they stare at each other and me with a look of

"What the heck is wrong with her???" I tell them I wouldn't have to yell if they had just listened the first three hundred and thirty-seven thousand times I asked. I then lay down the law again, followed with a new list of consequences. They again follow it for a short period of time...I ask again, blah, blah, blah......and so the cycle repeats itself. Sound familiar? Sure, your number might be different than three hundred and thirty-seven thousand (my kids pointed out to me that this is always the number I use when I'm mad), but either way, it is my guess that if you're a normal parent, with normal children, you most likely have a similar situation with its own variation of circumstances. I have to say that sometimes the frustration of it all simply impedes my sanity.

I should point out that I am a Pediatric RN with a Bachelor of Science Nursing degree. I have worked at a Children's Hospital for over fifteen years. In addition to my own parenting as a mother of six, I have gathered some experience through my career in regards to how children work and learn, as well as how they relate to authority and other children.

Over the years, I have tried multiple disciplines and chore plans. I have tried task lists, task boxes, behavior bucks, and clean room awards. You name it, I have tried it. None were effective for very long.

I wanted a plan that my children would not only follow but one they would appreciate and learn from. It is my job as their mother to help them become upstanding adults. I wanted to teach the children to recognize personal responsibility as it relates to themselves and those around them. Whether it is caring for themselves, cleaning up, doing chores, helping others or cleaning up garbage on the street. That is what the Respect Rocks Program is all about. Through love, recognize something needs to be done, and do it!

I do not profess to be an author or a professional writer. The intention of this book is not to be a perfectly written manuscript but rather my story in its simplistic form. I could have had a professional writer compose this for me but I didn't want to lose my story or program in the process.

I have spent about three years writing this book. During this time, I have been trying to find the *perfect* way to share my program and put it all into the *perfect* words and organization. Because perfection is difficult to attain, and because I am not a writer, I was never quite sure if my message was coming out the way I intended. This simply led to a cycle of never actually publishing or sharing my program.

My sweet husband finally pointed out to me that something was getting lost. He reminded me that my intention when I started this was never to make money or to create the perfect manuscript. It was rather to simply share my story and my amazing program with others. He helped me to understand that while I was spending so much time making it "perfect", people were ultimately missing out. Knowing that my true intentions are to help people, I knew that no matter what, it was time to publish my book.

So here it is in its purest form.

My story, my program, my system

My

"Respect Rocks"

Chapter 1:

Loving All: The Golden Rule and The Simplicity of "RESPECT"

Almost everyone has heard of "The Golden Rule". It is a concept that has been around for ages and practiced in many themes, religions and cultures. You don't have to be a philosopher or a religious person of any faith to have appreciation for the Golden Rule. Do unto others as you would have done unto you. It is actually quite basic and simple. I have learned that often simplicity is the best answer. Over-complicating can lead to being confused and over-whelmed which can lead to giving up all together.

As a health care provider I research many subjects. During my research I came across an interesting correlation between love for all mankind and near death experiences. Yes, I know; death, dying, and Respect Rocks, where is she going with this!? Hang on, it is a simple, pure, and beautiful concept.

Researchers consistently come to one underlying conclusion from the majority of near death experiences studied. They report that people who have had a near death experience have consistently reported waking up with an unprecedented focus on service, love and appreciation for all of mankind. Time after time, people have reported returning from near death with a pure love for all and a sincere desire to serve others. This tells me that somewhere inside each of us, is a deep, subconscious connection to others and a sincere ability for us all to love unconditionally.

Feeling a great energy in this, I wanted to teach my children to tap into this unconditional love for all people. I felt that sometimes all the rules of life got a little complicated but if I could at least teach them love and appreciation for others, I would have instilled something very important in them that they would utilize their entire life. Teaching kindness and love for those we share the world with, as well as having appreciation for the earth and all that it encompasses, creates an aura of energy that is so powerful. Yet in its simplistic form, even my youngest child, who was five years old at the time, could feel and understand its positive effects.

After coming to this realization that I needed to simplify and get back to the basics of pure love, it all seemed to come together quite nicely. I pondered for a long time. I was trying to figure out a way to incorporate this new found simplistic love for all into one plan that also addressed the discipline needed to rear my children. Through all of my ponderings, the magic word finally came to me. "RESPECT!" That was it! "RESPECT" encompassed it all.

It was so simple! If I could just teach the children to have respect for essentially everything, the rest would come naturally. I also knew that I would not be able to teach the children love and respect for others if they did not learn to love and respect themselves. Treating each other poorly definitely shows a lack of love and respect for each other but also shows a lack of love and respect for yourself. Not taking care of your stuff and home also shows a lack of respect for yourself. Willingly doing your chores is ultimately showing respect for your home. Keeping your home clean, shows respect for yourself as you develop the desire to not live in dirt, grime, filth, muck and disorder.

I also feel strongly that we as humans have, within our core elements, the sincere ability to empathize with others. For example, although I have never been physically tortured myself, if I watch a movie where this is happening to someone, I am able to empathize with them and feel heartbroken about their pain. Although I have never actually felt that kind of pain myself, there is something that is within me, outside of my own personal experience, which allows me to feel the empathy for the person who is suffering.

Another perfect example happened one day as I was talking with my children at the dinner table. We were talking about how everyone is an individual. To help them understand, I used a metaphor and compared people's diverse individual traits to their feet. I explained that everyone's feet are different sizes, widths, and textures for a reason. There are flat feet, skinny feet, fat feet, short feet, and long feet. There are people from different cultures who don't wear shoes thus creating thick calloused feet and, on the flip side, there are people who get weekly pedicures so their feet are nice and soft.

The reality is that the events and experiences of those people's lives have created the feet that they have. Therefore, you cannot expect them all to fit into one size of molded shoes. If we were all intended to fit into the same size shoes, then we would all have one size of feet with the same experiences for all of us.

I told my children to let their feet grow into whatever size was meant for them and don't allow someone else to put shoes on them that don't fit. I emphasized that they could become anything they wanted. I advised them not to allow other people's negativity and discouragement to keep them from evolving into the person they were meant to be.

I also explained, that they need to respect other people's "feet" and in turn, not try to force other people's "feet" into their shoes. I gave the example of Connor (age twelve at the time) trying to wear Jensen's shoes (age six at the time). As my analogy was making sense to the children, Connor began to joke that he would have to cut off his toes to fit into Jensen's shoes.

Later, Jensen said he just kept thinking about Connor having to cut off his toes and he said he felt like his own toes were being cut off and he could almost feel the pain of that. Jensen has never even remotely had his toes cut off or anything like it. He was six years old at the time and although his personal experiences did not support being able to feel the pain of having his toes cut off, he was able to actually feel the pain, just through thought. I commended him on his ability to recognize the specific empathy inside him. I explained this was the inherent trait within him that will help him truly connect with other people in the world and help him to anticipate their needs through intention. Although I believe we all initially have this amazing innate gift, I think that sometimes it just gets overrun with the ways and stresses of life. We almost become immune and unable to tap in to what was originally there to begin with.

Because I believe so strongly in this, I wanted to provide an opportunity for my children to feel and hopefully comprehend the innate sense of truly feeling what others feel. I also wanted to teach them the importance of being able to step out of yourself and out of your own arrogance for a few moments to grasp what it really means to help others and to do the right thing.

They needed to learn to do things, not because they expect something or recognition in return but because their innate sense tells them to do it. Not because they live in fear of punishment but because they recognize the positive standards they are setting within themselves as a more gratifying, as well as self-reliant way to engage the world. Giving because you expect to get something back, isn't really giving. That is simply providing advanced payment for what you expect in return. Giving is an entirely different concept and is dependent on complete selflessness. Mastering the ability to selflessly recognize and anticipate the needs of the people and situations around you is key. Seeing this ability, as imperative for your own growth, is where I believe one of the highest levels of personal achievement can be attained. This was my underlying goal of the "Respect Rocks" program.

Chapter 2:

The RESPECT ROCKS Program

Once I had figured out the purpose and goal of the program, I needed to incorporate an incentive plan. How would I keep track of things, and what exactly would the children earn?

Many people use allowance as an incentive plan and I have differing views and mixed opinions on this. Some people say that kids should get allowance because it is a good incentive for them to do their chores. Others say that they should not get money for doing everyday chores because chores are a part of their duty as a member of the family. Following that, others will argue that as a member of the family, doing everyday chores for the family earns them part of the family income. Professionals could argue about this topic forever and never really come up with the "right" solution. For me, I had tried every avenue with allowance and nothing really seemed to fit.

Even before Respect Rocks, I have always felt that I needed an incentive for my kids to do their chores but I didn't think that it was right to teach them that they were always going to get paid money for doing a task that was already their responsibility in the first place. It seemed however to leave them unwilling to do it if they were not going to get paid. This was far from my goal or intention of teaching them to be upstanding adults.

I also had my own personal issue of having actual cash available to pay them every week. In a world that has become so dependent on computer transactions and debit cards, I rarely have cash on hand and I rarely make a trip to the bank. Additionally, bank ATMs are not much help as they only deliver $20 bills. So I was faced with another issue of actually paying out the money that my children earned weekly and as you can imagine, this was not the best system for a mother who struggled with follow through.

I even tried using fake money (Monopoly money) and behavior bucks. It was just fake money or pieces of paper that no one realistically viewed as real money, so they were not treated as such. I was constantly finding the bucks lying all over the place. They were easy to lose and easy to replace, which didn't make for a very valuable system.

Although I didn't have great luck with any system for allowance, I still needed a reasonable incentive for my newfound program. The kids needed to learn work ethic and responsibility. I knew to be realistic, there needed to be an incentive plan if I wanted to be successful and better yet, if I wanted the children to learn to become successful themselves.

You may be thinking this idea of an incentive plan is a complete contradiction to the previous chapter's concept of encouraging the children to learn to do things because they want to and not because they are being rewarded. Please remember that we are dealing with children who are still very easily molded and are in essence, waiting for their adult models to show them the way to create their own patterns. This doesn't at all discount or overshadow the natural ability to love and care that already exists inside them. I believe that sometimes they need things initially pointed out to them so that they will be able to eventually recognize it on their own. Providing initial incentives simply creates a chain of positive reinforcement. Based on the laws of cause and effect, this will in turn help them become more reliant on themselves and their own instincts.

This is the core meaning of my quote that I presented at the beginning of this book. *"Respect is not given, it is earned. Respect is not innate, it is learned."* We are all born with the natural ability to love. I truly believe it is a part of us. Respect on the other hand is not innate but is rather a learned extension of the love that is within us. Just as we ourselves have to earn the respect of others, we also can learn to respect our entire environment. This includes all the people, animals, objects and elements that exist with in it, including ourselves. Learning to live your life with respect for all of these things creates a thought process that has a snowball of positive effects. In essence, I want to teach the children to channel this *innate* love into a *learned* respect.

My Respect Rocks program creates the bridge or conduit for this to happen. At first the behavior is recognized and rewarded but after a while the pattern of respect is created within the children and they are able to continue moving forward based on their own positive energy instincts. I have already seen this in my own children. They often do the things that earn them Respect Rocks yet they never ask for the rocks. They simply do it because they have learned to do it and because they know what is expected; and they do it without thinking about it. They also have begun recognizing the patterns of respect in situations that are not things that I have specifically told them about. They are grasping these ideas of respect in all facets of their lives including ones outside our home and outside of themselves.

With this outcome, my goal is ultimately attained and the behavior patterns that they learn to recognize in their childhood will hopefully follow them into adulthood. My end goal is to help them recognize the behavior and how it makes them feel as well as recognize the positive chain of events that it sets in motion. I believe that it will become instinctual and second nature. I want them to understand that who they are when they think no one is watching, is the person that their true individual spirit of self really is.

RESPECT ROCKS: A "Point" System

In my continued ponderings about a functional and effective behavior program, I decided that some sort of "point" system would work and that a point system using marbles or rocks in a jar would be ideal! The kids could earn "rocks" for all the big things like chores such as bathrooms, vacuuming, dusting, cleaning rooms etc. They could also earn rocks for all the little things as well, such as putting their toothbrush away, cleaning up their plates after meals, putting hair ties away after the shower, etc.

I also liked the idea of the immediate recognition and reinforcement that is created with a personal accumulating "good deed" rock jar. The daily payoff is very visible and the amount of rocks that could be building is limitless. The kids would get immediate positive reinforcement for everything they did, or immediate negative reinforcement as well. Either way, it is a quick way to instantly reinforce their behavior.

Initially, I wasn't sure how to create the "list" of what I wanted the kids to do on a regular basis. I have tried using "task lists" before and you probably have too. Tasks lists can be effective in some areas and completely ineffective in others. Although it works great for well-defined chores (as long as there are consequences and follow through), I found that it doesn't do much for helping my kids to be responsible for the everyday individual items that they would fail to do like cleaning up their place at the dinner table, putting away their tooth brush, cleaning up their clothes and hair ties after their bath...etc.

Even if the task list is more generic and only mentions "picking up after yourself", and earning a "check" that day for doing so, I found that the kids would often get somewhat impartial to it because it was all or nothing. If they saw that they had more than just a few things out, then they just opted to forget about it all together thus loosing the "check" for that day; because after all, it was only one check.

The other option was to put every single task down on the list. However that would lead to a pretty lengthy list, which can be overwhelming for kids. It is very time consuming to write everything down and if your life is like mine, new tasks are constantly being added, as well as new items being left out. Also if you do forget something, and leave it off the list, kids translate that into not needing to do it. You end up having to be pretty specific with the list. So I found that with task lists, the problem of having their stuff left out wasn't solved on a daily basis and they weren't learning a lot of self-responsibility.

I felt they needed a plan that sort of encompassed everything and more importantly taught them to think for themselves about the tasks that were their responsibility. Task list were great to a point but I wanted the children thinking beyond what was laid out in black and white on a list.

More importantly, I was having a difficult time trying to teach them respect for each other, and tasks lists didn't do much to help solve this problem. The fighting and arguing was ridiculous and someone always ended up in tears; especially our fifth child Haedyn. She has two older brothers and one younger brother. It seemed that she was always the one getting picked on. The infamous "target" of all the pranks, jokes and ridicule. Her place in the age line-up of children makes her an easy target. She is also a bit of a drama queen so getting her worked up is easy, and the boys all worked together to monopolize on this. Although task lists could be effective for individual chores, they did nothing to promote harmony, unity and love within our home or between the children.

I then realized that if I created a point/rock system to accommodate chores, task lists and taking personal responsibility for your stuff, why not incorporate a rock system for being nice, kind, and helpful to each other.

The kids could earn rocks for being kind and helpful to each other as well as feeding the dog and helping me with the younger kids etc. Just as they could lose rocks for not doing their chores, they would more importantly lose rocks for being mean to each other.

If they didn't do their chores, they would give rocks to me. But if the kids were mean to each other, they would have to give the rocks out of their jar, to the person that they were mean to. I thought that would be the ultimate consequence! Not only would they be losing a rock for being mean to their sibling but they would actually be increasing the rocks for the sibling they were mean to. This would put them behind by one rock and in-turn put the sibling ahead by a rock. Therefore the lack of respect for the sibling actually put them behind that sibling by two rocks. Brilliant!!

I then took my thoughts one step further. I could extend the love and generosity outside of our home. The kids would be encouraged to help others at school or the neighbors or pick up trash on the way home from school. I realized there were no limits to how far we could go with this new plan of love and respect that was quickly developing within my mind, heart & soul.

RESPECT ROCKS: The Incentive

I had to figure out what the true incentive would be. What would the kids get if they earned the most rocks? Earlier, I discussed the pros and cons of allowance. The Respect Rocks program closes this gap and creates a system where the children can actually earn money for earning the most rocks. That way they are actually earning what they get paid. I initially liked the idea of all or nothing, especially since it was a competition. So when I started, I decided that the "prize" would be a $50 bill, given to the winner at the end of the competition. You can obviously adjust this to any amount that is suitable for your family.

I want to point out that the award can be anything and certainly doesn't have to be money. Money just worked for our family because it solved the allowance issue. However, you could award privileges instead of money. For example, maybe your kids fight over who gets to ride in the front seat of the car. The winner could get to ride shotgun for a week. Maybe the winner could have control over the TV for a week, stay up an extra thirty min later than the other children or maybe additional video game time. You could make the competition only last for a week. Each new week a new competition would begin and the winner could get to choose what award they wanted for the following week. Really, the options are limitless and creating a system that is specific to your family is what is going to be a key component to its success.

Even if you only have one child, Respect Rocks can still be used as a behavior modification program. Instead of a competition between multiple children, the reward can be individualized for that one child, based on what incentive works best for him/ her. Set the reward in advance and the number of rocks needed to attain that reward. Your child will still enjoy the feeling of immediate recognition as their personal jar fills up, as well as the accomplishment when they earn the reward.

RESPECT ROCKS: The Four Main Ideas of Respect

As I created the system, I broke it down into the four most important ideas that I wanted the children to learn. I knew simplicity was going to be the key but I also needed it to encompass everything to allow for its growth and evolution. The four ideas are: Respect for SELF, Respect for OTHERS, Respect for HOME, and Respect for EARTH/UNIVERSE.

SELF is where children can focus on loving and caring for themselves and their bodies. From brushing their teeth or taking a bath to choosing a healthy snack over an unhealthy one, they can earn Respect Rocks. I teach my children to respect their bodies and to take pride in caring for it. They can also earn rocks for remembering to take their medication or doing their homework. Anything that has to do with their personal responsibilities falls under this category.

Respect for OTHERS is pretty self-explanatory and so many rocks can be earned this way. Helping someone out with homework, being kind, sharing a snack or opening a door. The list for helping OTHERS is truly endless.

Respect for HOME pretty much incorporates all of the things that we own and should take care of; our home, rooms, cars, shoes, socks, toys, games etc. This is also where all the chores and house cleaning comes in. It is the "productive" side of Respect Rocks. My house has never been cleaner and my kids often fight over who gets to do what chore. The point of Respect Rocks is obviously to keep them from fighting but I have to say that I don't mind a few arguments about who "gets" to clean the toilets!

Respect for EARTH/ UNIVERSE gives the children a focal point that is greater than themselves. Allowing them to grasp the idea that we are all only one small intricate part of a greater system. Having the ability to think outside of yourself on a larger scale creates a greater awareness of how we all work together for the good of mankind. It also allows for respect of things like recycling, not being wasteful and appreciating our beautiful earth that needs to be cared for.

RESPECT ROCKS: Preparation

1. LARGE POSTER BOARD

2. CUP, GLASS OR CONTAINER FOR EACH CHILD WITH THEIR NAME WRITTEN ON IT

3. GLASS ROCKS (accent gems for planters and vases, or any other small item that can be placed in jars. One friend of mine used pinto beans!)

4. THIRTY MINUITES UNINTERUPTED DISCUSSION TIME WITH THE FAMILY

To start my preparation, I got a large poster board and wrote the word "RESPECT" at the top, followed with the definition: "An attitude of admiration or esteem". I then numbered the important areas. Below I have listed the areas that I use but you can replace it with whatever suits your goals or needs.

1) Respect for SELF

2) Respect for OTHERS

3) Respect for HOME

4) Respect for EARTH/ UNIVERSE

After over three years of following this plan, I have found that for my family, these four things seem to encompass everything. Everything can fall into one of these four simple categories. What's great about this system is that you can adjust the parameters to whatever ideals you choose to teach your children and whatever suits your family's specific needs. You can add things where you may feel you need to be more specific. If you follow an organized religion or belief system, you may want to incorporate something specific as it relates to your religion and beliefs. Either way, adjusting the system to fit your personal needs is very easy. Although I firmly believe that simplicity is the core of this system, individual interpretation is what makes the world go round so it is easy to modify it to your own needs and specifications.

After I made my poster board, I went to the dollar store and purchased glass vases or containers; one for each child and one for myself. With a sharpie, I wrote each child's name on his/her container. I also had my own jar with "Mom/ Dad" written on it. I do not actually earn rocks myself but this jar is where the children put the rocks that they lose. I also purchased "accent gems". They are the stones that are used in vases for floral arrangements and decorating. They are simple little blue stones but to us, they are now called "Respect Rocks".

Chapter 3:

Introducing "RESPECT ROCKS" To the Children

Now I have to say, introducing the new plan to the kids was one of the best parts. We had a lot of fun that day. In our home, we did a thing on Monday nights called Family Night. I introduced my newfound system to the children during June of 2009, so they were out of school at the time. My husband's children Brielle and Jack, were in California with their mom, so the first competition was just with the four children living in our home full time; Marissa, Connor, Haedyn and Jensen. Monday morning, I told the kids I had something exciting planned for Family Night. My kids love Family Night, so at this point, I had already got their attention. I told them they had to do their chores first and clean their rooms during the day to be completely ready for Family Night.

As they were doing their chores, I went around saying for example "Oh, Haedyn gets one for R3" if she had completed a chore (Respect for HOME), or "Connor gets one for R2" if he did something to help another sibling out (Respect for OTHERS). Or "Jensen gets one for R1" if he remembered to brush his teeth without being reminded (Respect for SELF). This went on the entire day. I have to say that I was quite generous with giving out rocks that first day as it only increased their motivation and curiosity. They were giddy with excitement and going crazy trying to figure out what I was talking about and the enthusiasm for the night amplified throughout the day. They were beside themselves by the end of the day anticipating what they had earned as they wondered what on earth I was talking about.

This was the only day that I ever specified "R1, R2, R3" or "R4" as they earned rocks. I did this only for the sake of introducing the system because the children had no idea what I was doing. Since then, there has been no reason to specify as the children are well aware what they are earning and losing rocks for. Making a numbered list of the Respect goals in the beginning is more about giving them a general idea of certain important focal points.

Throughout the day, I kept totals of how many "Respect Rocks" each child had earned. I placed the correct number of rocks that each child earned in his/her personalized jar. That night, when it came time for the presentation and introduction of "Respect Rocks", I placed each child's jar on the table in the family room.

I began the night by explaining to them that throughout the day, they were already earning rocks. I let them make guesses of what they thought was going on. They had some close guesses as to what they were specifically earning rocks for such as doing chores or helping others, but they didn't figure out the system as a whole. I then showed them the poster that I had made with the four different aspects of respect that they were going to be accountable for. I told them that we were getting back to basics and I really felt that creating love and respect in all they do was a vital key to their personal growth.

I went on to explain that to make it more fun and exciting, they would be in competition with each other and only one person would get the grand prize. I had one envelope that had the word "RESPECT" written in huge red letters on it. Contained in the envelope was a $50 bill, which would be the prize. I revealed what was in the envelope at the end of the night. Waiting to see what was in the envelope helped to keep the children's anticipation growing throughout the night.

Once they learned about the new plan of Respect Rocks, they were all very excited. From the fourteen year old down to the five year old, I had their attention. I explained to them, the many different ways that they would earn rocks and ways that they would lose rocks and I told them that some would be automatic. "Automatic" rocks included picking up their place after dinner, cleaning up their clothes after a shower, putting their towel back after the shower, putting away the toothbrush and toothpaste, remembering to take their allergy medication, etc. If they did these things, then they would automatically earn the rocks and if they didn't do them, then they would automatically lose the rocks.

Teamwork:

While teaching the children to complete individual tasks and chores, I also wanted to simultaneously teach teamwork. I wanted them to learn to work together to keep the house clean and encourage the children to help each other earn rocks as well.

In addition to the children earning rocks for directly helping others with tasks such as homework and cleaning up their rooms, I also let them earn rocks for nicely reminding one of their siblings to complete a task.

For example if Haedyn left her clothes in the bathroom after the bath, Jensen could put the clothes away and earn a rock. He would earn a rock and Haedyn wouldn't lose any because ultimately the task was completed. However, if Jensen nicely reminded Haedyn to put her clothes away, Haedyn would earn the rock for putting the clothes away. In turn, Jensen would earn two rocks for going the extra mile to help a sibling out as well as keeping respect for our home by making sure the task was completed. The kids almost always choose to nicely remind each other of the task because ultimately they earn one more rock than if they had simply done the task themselves.

I recognize that it is obviously good practice to sometimes simply do things for others. However, at this point of the learning experience, I want the kids to learn to work together and not just leave their responsibilities to others because they know someone else will come along and do it for them. Additionally, I don't want them to feel that their success is earned by allowing others to slack in their responsibilities. I like this because it helps the kids remind each other of each person's own responsibilities and facilitates continuity between the children as well as the tasks in our home. I also feel that helping the children to learn to work with others is crucial for success in life.

The kids ultimately do not like being told what to do by their siblings and they don't like that their own neglect gave opportunity for their sibling to earn two rocks. So it actually encourages them more to put their own stuff away, before their sibling has a chance to tell them to do it.

I also decided that it was important for the kids to be the ones to tell me when they earned the rocks. I figured this was another way to teach them responsibility and I thought that it kept it fair in case I missed something that one of them had done. So, they were responsible for doing the task as well as putting their rocks in their jars after they had told me that they had completed the task. They were not allowed to put the rocks in their jars until they told me, so that I could still keep track of what they were earning rocks for. They were additionally responsible for physically putting the rocks in my jar if they lost one.

I felt that this was an effective way for them to take responsibility for themselves, which is the purpose of the system. I told them that if I found out that they had not done something that they said they did, then they would lose double the rocks that they would have earned.

I have had many people tell me that their kids would be dishonest and sneak extra rocks in the jars when the parents weren't looking. My response is that their kids are obviously in need of a system that teaches respect!

Although I have never encountered dishonesty like that with the Respect Rock jars, I have had a child lie to me during a competition. It was a little insignificant lie and had nothing to do with Respect Rocks, but nevertheless, it was a lie. So consequently, that child had to take their rock jar, dump it out completely and start from scratch. It was an important lesson for that child as well as the other children. The great thing is that now, the child that lied, is often reminding the other children in advance, that they need to just be honest and that no matter what, lying about it is much more painful. My children know that I am totally intolerant of lying and that dishonesty negates all their other good deeds. This consequence teaches that with out trust, nothing else matters.

If you are already starting with dishonest children then there are ways to address this and protect the jars from being falsely accessed. My suggestion is to keep the jars locked up in a chest or the parent's room. The parents and kids can keep track of the rocks earned daily on a piece of paper or notebook. Then take five minutes at the end of the night where the jars come out and the rocks are awarded or taken away for the day's tasks. Then lock the jars back up until the following day. The kids will look forward to the time they get to award their rocks and there will be no opportunity for upping their rocks without the parent's knowledge.

I personally was not too worried about my children cheating and putting extra rocks in their jars because I warned them that if they did this, they would automatically be out of the competition and would be on "Plan B". That was enough to keep them honest. After three years of doing the plan now, I have never encountered a problem with this. What is this "Plan B" I speak of? I am so glad you asked!

Chapter 4:

"Plan B"

To this day, my children still cringe when they hear "Plan B". Yet for me, "Plan B" holds a very special place in my heart. This plan was developed before Respect Rocks and after ultimate frustration of the kids not doing what I asked. It is definitely the precursor to the development of Respect Rocks and I still use it as a back up system. If the kids give any opposition to Respect Rocks or quit trying, they know that the alternative is going back to "Plan B".

About a year before the creation of Respect Rocks, I decided that if the children weren't willing to do what I asked and expected of them, then I was not willing to do what they asked and expected of me.

This plan originated when I was trying out the allowance idea of "everyone is part of the family so everyone is part of the work and in turn, everyone is part of the fun". I equated this plan with that of the real world. I explained that I had to go to work to earn the money to pay for the things that I wanted. That was how the real world worked, so the kids needed to learn this expectation as well.

The idea was to teach the children that they had to do their part to get their part. I explained to them that as their mother, I was only required to give them food, shelter and clothes as far as physical necessities were concerned. Other than that, they were on their own. I had no obligation to provide toys, games, TV, bikes, scooters or rides to the mall or movies with friends, trips snow-skiing, or to Disneyland.

I advised the children that they either did their part or they would be on "Plan B". To get them to fully understand "Plan B", I explained to them "Plan A". "Plan A" was "A+ attitude". Doing things when I asked, helping others, picking up after themselves etc. "Plan A" integrated it all and was more of a general plan. If they did what they were asked, when they were asked, then I would do my part. I would buy them things, take them places, allow them use of all the fun things that we had at home such as the trampoline, video games, TV, motor scooters etc. I was hopeful that the kids would just be able to figure it out themselves. That they would have the integrity to do their part and in turn, they would be able to get the things that they desired and go to the places they wanted to go, like the movies, ice skating, Disneyland, etc.

They would also continue to have full access to all the fun things that we had around the house. Such as, the Jacuzzi, the trampoline, computer, games, satellite TV, the Playstation, the Wii, the projector, their bikes, scooters, electric Razor scooters, power wheels toys...etc. Basically, we would all work together, in a perfect give and take manner and we would all sit around together in harmony singing *Kumbaya*, with birds chirping along to the melody. Ya... right!!

This is where "Plan B" comes in. "Plan B" is the exact opposite of "Plan A". With "Plan A", the kids already had everything, they just needed to do what it took to maintain it. With "Plan B", instead of me freely giving to the children and them having free rein of all of their toys, games etc, they would have nothing and had to earn and pay for everything that they used or wanted to do. (Other than food, clothing, and shelter, etc.) I informed the kids that they did not owe me anything. They could sit around the house as slugs but in turn, they would not be able to have anything until they earned it. My thoughts were that they would quickly learn that it was pretty boring sitting around with nothing to do or play with. Additionally, having to pay for everything was going to get quickly expensive on a child's ability to earn an income. My hopes were that they would be able to see how lucky they were to have everything they were given, appreciate it and reciprocate the generosity. Did it work? You will soon find out.

When first introducing this plan to the children, I was quite specific. I am a firm believer that children should be well aware in advance of consequences. That way they can take full responsibility if their choices bring them those consequences. I explained to the kids the specifics of "Plan B". With this plan, the kids would have nothing beyond their physical needs. They literally had to pay for everything. If they wanted to go somewhere, they had to pay $1 each way. If we went to the movies as a family, they not only had to pay for the movie, they also had to pay $1 each way to get to and from the movie. Unless of course they wanted to walk, which was not an option in their eyes. For safety reasons, I would never really let them do that, so paying for a ride and earning the money for that ride was really the only option. I also broke down what it would cost to rent their toys or to purchase them outright.

For example, if the trampoline cost $300, each child had to come up with $50 to purchase his/her portion of the trampoline. Or they could rent it for $5 per month. It also costs $2400 for our screen TV and an additional $80 per month for satellite TV. So I figured it was about $300 per person to purchase their portion of the TV (since the adults watched it too, it was divided by 8) or about $20 per month to rent it. Then they would have to pay for their portion of the satellite, which was an additional $10 per month, totaling $30 per month for the use of the TV with satellite. They also had to pay for their electric scooters, which were each about $200, or rent them for $4 per month. They could also pay for the Playstation and Wii but then they had to pay for each individual game as well.

They could earn money for what they wanted by doing chores around the house. For example cleaning the bathrooms, wiping down baseboards, taking out the trash, etc. However, earning money for each individual chore wasn't worth much. Even doing all the chores didn't get them enough money to pay for everything they already had when they were on "Plan A". As I expected, they quickly learned, just by talking about it, that "Plan B" was not fun and was very expensive. "Plan A", on the other hand, was a much better plan.

Plan B: The manual

My friend told me about a story of her husband growing up. His mother supposedly showed him and his siblings only once, how to do a chore. Take for instance, cleaning the bathroom. She would show them how to clean it in a fashion that was satisfactory to her. They would then do it themselves and she would check it when they were done. If they had not done it to her satisfaction or in the way that she had shown them, she would simply state, "Nope, do it again". They would then have to start from scratch until it met her satisfaction. She would also not tell them what was wrong with it because she had already told them how to do it once, so why should she need to repeat herself. To me, as a person who was sick to death of always having to repeat myself three hundred and thirty-seven thousand times, this was music to my ears. The idea of only saying something once?!?!.... Fabulous!!

After I thought about it though, I realized that my kids aren't great listeners and there would be a good chance that they would truly not have any idea what part of the bathroom needed to be redone. I then pictured myself spending all day Saturday saying "Nope, do it again", "Nope, do it again", "Nope, do it again". I would just be repeating myself over and over; which was the exact thing that I was trying to avoid. I also pictured my kids whaling and crying on the bathroom floor, which would of course not be clean. Being the germ-a-phobe that I am, and being opposed to the idea of my children rolling around on the dirty, aseptic bathroom floor, I decided that I needed to make a few adjustments to this new strategy.

So I decided to put together a manual. Included in the manual was an exact, precise description of how I expected the children to do their chores. That way, when they weren't sure what they had done wrong or what they had missed with cleaning, they would all be able to refer to their manual. Each child received their very own copy to keep in their rooms. It was a neatly bound folder with each page in its own page protector. I titled the manual, "The What To Do, When To Do and How To Do It Manual: A Guide to Staying Off Plan B." The manual also gave specifics about how the chore needed to be done everyday versus the deeper cleaning that needed to be done on Saturdays.

The following is what was contained in "The Manual":

The What To Do, When To Do and How To Do It Manual: A Guide to Staying Off "Plan B"

BEDROOMS

Daily

1. Bed made.
2. Clothes in hamper.
3. Old water cup from the night before, taken to kitchen sink/ dishwasher before getting a new one.
4. Nothing left on floors.
5. Picked up prior to going to bed and prior to going to school.

Saturday

6. #1, 2, 3, 4 & 5 from above.
7. Closet cleaned out, shoes organized.
8. Dresser cleaned off AND organized.
9. Dust/ wipe down.
10. Garbage that has collected ANYWHERE in room be thrown away.

BEDTIME/ BATHTIME RITUAL

1. Bedtime on school nights is 8:30pm SHARP! Bedtime on weekends is 9:00pm SHARP. Bedtime means in bed with lights off. Homework complete and bedtime rituals already complete. For example: Already gone to the bathroom, already have drinks and already told mom whatever it is you need to tell her from the day.
2. Prior to going to bed, the family room, playroom and bedrooms must be picked up.
3. For every minute past 8:30pm, double the time will be deducted from bedtime the following night.
4. If you are unable to get up in the morning when you are told, bedtime will be changed to an earlier time.
5. Showers and baths are to be started at 7pm. (Unless we are not home yet)
   a. After shower/bath, ALL CLOTHES, SHOES, HAIR TIES, OR ANYTHING ELSE THAT WAS BROUGHT/ PUT INTO THE BATHROOM AS A RESULT OF THE SHOWER RITUAL, SHALL BE PICKED UP AND PUT IN THE APPROPRIATE PLACE!!!!!! NO EXCEPTIONS!!!!
   b. Brush and floss teeth. Use mouthwash. Put everything back after you are done.
6. If you are able to get all of the above bedtime requirements completed prior to bedtime, you are free to spend the left over time until bedtime as you choose.
7. If you are successful with bedtime throughout the week, a late night can be earned for the weekend.

CLEANING THE BATHROOMS

FULL CLEANING

1. Remove items from counter.
2. Use Soft Scrub on counters, sink and faucet. Squirt small to moderate amount on counters. Using a wet washcloth and a circular motion, buff soft scrub onto counters, sink AND drain, removing dirt and grime.
3. Rinse washcloth with water and wipe wet washcloth on counter and sinks.
4. Repeat step 3 until soap is removed.
5. Dry sink and countertops with dry towel.
6. Clean mirrors with Windex and paper towels. Repeat until ALL streaks and spots are off mirror.
7. Step back and look at mirror from ALL angles to assure that ALL spots and streaks have been removed.
8. Repeat step 7, because there is a good chance there are still spots and streaks.
9. Put toilet cleaner in toilet. Let sit while cleaning ENTIRE toilet with antibacterial wipes. Use one wipe for outer toilet (everything but seat), and one wipe to clean the top of the seat and THEN under seat....in that order.
10. Use antibacterial wipes to wipe down counter items and place them NICELY and ORDERLY on counter.

PARTIAL CLEANING

1. Using antibacterial wipes, wipe down counter, faucet, sink and drain.
2. Toilet may also need a wipe down with antibacterial wipes. Do this as needed. (If you think there is any chance that mom will think it is needed, then it is.)

***Full cleaning to be done every Saturday by ALL children.

***Partial cleaning to be done:

        Monday: Mom

        Tuesday: Marissa

        Wednesday: Haedyn

        Thursday: Connor

VACUUMING

1. For the new carpets in the family room, living room, and parent's room, vacuum should be placed on "CARPET" setting and "carpet height" should be set in the middle.
2. For the kid's rooms and playroom, change "carpet height" to the lowest setting.
3. For the tile, the setting should be placed on "tile" and the "carpet height" to the lowest setting.
4. A systematic approach should be done while vacuuming to assure that all areas are covered. This is more difficult to tell on the tile. Thus a systematic approach of "tile by tile" or "line by line" aids in this process. This is also helpful when vacuuming the carpet as you will see the lines where you have and have not vacuumed.
5. If the vacuum will not get something especially along the baseboards, detach the suction hose and vacuum along the baseboard.
6. ALL kitchen chairs and barstools should be moved and area under table and bar vacuumed.
7. If there is something in the way or on the floor that is inhibiting you from vacuuming, move it and/or put it away and proceed with vacuuming. Do not just leave the item there and vacuum around it.

CAR

1. If you bring it into the car it is your responsibility to get it out.
2. If you fail to get any item that you brought into the car, out of the car, you will no longer be able to bring items into the car and this may result in losing that item.
3. Garbage needs to be picked up daily. This includes wrappers, cups, drinks etc.
4. Car is to be cleaned on Saturday mornings. This includes vacuuming and wiping down the inside. Washing the outside.
5. If it becomes a problem for anyone to leave items in the car, trash in the car or disrespecting the car, that person will loose the FREE privilege of getting rides in the car and will be charged an appropriate fee for receiving rides in the car to and from their activities.

HOMEWORK

1. Homework shall be started at 4 pm sharp.
2. If scouts, gymnastics, sports, or any other conflicting preplanned afternoon activity, then homework shall be started immediately after school, or immediately after returning form the activity.
3. You are welcome to start homework earlier if preferred.
4. If we are not home at the above stated times, homework shall be started immediately upon arrival home or can be done in the car.
5. Homework shall be completed before playing outside, watching TV, playing video games, or doing any other free-time activities.
6. YOUR homework is YOUR responsibility.
7. It is not mom or dad's responsibility to hound you, nag you, or remind you of your homework.

LAUNDRY

1. Put away all clothes in baskets. Connor and Jack help Jensen. Marissa and Brielle help Haedyn.
2. Clothes should be folded and put away in the appropriate places. NOT just shoved in the drawers.
3. Hang shirts and other hanging items on appropriate hangers AND hang up in closets. Mom will hang Dad's pants.
4. Socks should be folded and put in individual drawers. NOT left in sock bin.
5. Put Dad/ Mom's basket in their room.
6. Remaining hangers should be hung back in laundry room.
7. Pick up lint, wrappers and other laundry trash and put in garbage.
8. Put used dryer sheets in garbage.
9. Laundry NOT complete until all remnants of laundry is put in its appropriate place.

***Laundry is done on Monday's and whenever else Mom says

SET-UP & CLEAN-UP OF DINNER/ DISHES

<u>Before dinner</u>

1. Set table with napkin, fork, and drink for each person. Add spoon and knife if needed.
2. Make sure table is clean prior to setting. If it is not clean, wipe it off well with washcloth. Use antibacterial cleaner if needed. Remember, you will be eating off this table. Germs left on table will end up in your mouth when you eat.

<u>After dinner</u>

1. Clean off dishes in sink with water and sponge and place in orderly fashion in dishwasher.

2. If unable to put in dishwasher, large pots and pans should be cleaned WELL with soap and water. With the exception of all STONE-ware of which Mom will do.

3. Dry the dishes from step #2 with a fresh, CLEAN towel.

4. Once all possible dishes are placed in dishwasher, fill both chambers in dishwasher with correct dishwashing soap. Close lid on first chamber. Close dishwasher and press start.

5.   Wipe off countertops with wet washcloth until clean. Wipe down with kitchen antibacterial cleaner and paper towels or antibacterial wipes.

***All above listed tasks should be done by all available children, working together as a team.

****INABILITY TO WORK TOGETHER AS A TEAM, such as BICKERING, COMPLAINING OR FIGHTING IS CAUSE FOR IMMEDIATE DISMISAL TO BED FOR THE EVENING. (*My kids hate the idea of going to bed early so this was a big deal*)

TAKING OUT THE TRASH

1. Collect trash in trash bag. If not too full, the bag from the trash in parent's room can be used to collect trash from the smaller trash cans.

2. This includes collecting all trash that is surrounding trash can that has somehow not managed to make it into the actual trash can.

3. Be sure to collect trash from ALL cans including but not limited to: the kitchen, playroom, both bathrooms, kids rooms and parents room.

4. Make sure all trash is removed from the bottom of the can and be sure that can is empty. (Even if it means using your hands to remove the trash from the bottom of the can.)

5. A new garbage bag should be placed in ALL the cans. The kitchen can as well as the can in parent's rooms requires a large white bag. The smaller cans require a grocery sack as a trash liner.

6. Once all trash is collected, take it outside to the large black garbage can. DO NOT PUT IT ON THE SIDE OF THE LARGE BLACK TRASH CAN!! Actually put it IN the large black trash can.

7. WASH YOUR HANDS.....WITH SOAP!

*** Kitchen trash should be taken out daily and other cans should be taken out weekly at minimum.

***All trash may need to be taken out more frequently than previously mentioned and should be checked DAILY and taken out as needed.

***If it is full and/or overflowing, take it out using the above mentioned process.

***Even if you think it is not full and overflowing, there is a good chance it is........so empty it anyways.

GENERAL FAMILY RULES

1. If you get it out, put it back and/ or clean it up.
2. If you break it, fix it or you are responsible for replacing it.
3. Clean up after yourself. NO one here is hired as your personal maid.
4. Do what Mom or Dad ask the first time. You have ears. Use them to listen the first time.
5. Be kind to each other.
6. Name calling and hitting or pushing will NOT be tolerated.

END OF MANUAL

This manual worked great. It really helped to spell things out for the children. There were no more excuses for not knowing exactly what I expected, and that a half way job just wasn't going to cut it anymore.

Prior to initiating my original Manual, I also had the idea of showing the kids examples of doing things "half way". For dinner one night, I was going to throw a slab of uncooked meat on the table with some frozen vegetables. When they gave me their looks of "Huh??" my response would be, "Oh, you wanted me to cook it too? I thought I could squeak by, only completing the task half-way and just getting it out and putting it on the table."

I also considered getting them all excited about a new movie that had come out. We would get in the car, go to the theater, buy the tickets, then turn around and leave. I figured giving them great examples of the disappointment that comes from only completing a task half way would certainly create an impact on them. Although the thought of following through with these ideas certainly made me chuckle, I ultimately decided to first try "Plan B" and the accompanying manual. Looking back I am glad I did as it worked quite well and had the lasting impression I had hoped for. It also led right into Respect Rocks and is still an intricate part of our family.

At the end of this book, I have included a generic and customizable version of this Manual that you can use for your own family. You can fill in the blanks, add to it, and customize it for your personal family needs. I have left empty lines at the end of each section for your additions and modifications. There are also blank "task" pages for you to add your own personalized tasks. Fill it in as you see fit, or simply use it as a reference template for creating your own personalized manual. Either way, keep a manual available for your kids so they will know exactly what is expected of them.

Chapter 5:

The Tester Child; Is She Really Serious About "Plan B"??

Although just the thought of "Plan B" was somewhat terrifying to the children, there is always the one child who has to try it out to really get the full impact. That was my son Connor. He was nine years old at the time. His attitude was horrible. He was obsessed with video games and for some reason had developed a very entitled attitude. He had no desire to do anything other than watch TV, or play video games. If you dared to interrupt him during his video game time, you were quickly met with an attitude that lashed out with disgust and irritation. In fact, if you asked him to do anything, whether he was playing games or not, you were met with an attitude of disgust and irritation.

I had been threatening "Plan B" for about a month at this point and I think the threat of it had worn off. One particular day, Connor was playing video games and I asked him to stop and take out the trash. He rolled his eyes and gave an obviously irritated sigh. He paused his video game and took out the trash. However, he failed to put a new sack in the can. If you refer to the "TAKING OUT THE TRASH" section in the previously mentioned manual, you will see that step #5 clearly states to replace the garbage sack with a new one. So this particular day, after taking out the trash, Connor did not replace the bag.

Instead, he quickly went back to his game. I said, "Uh...Connor, you are not finished with the trash." He then threw down his arms, rolled his eyes, followed by his entire body, and let out the biggest grunt and sigh of frustration. I said "That's it...don't bother...you're officially on Plan B!"

He was shocked at first. He couldn't believe I was actually going to follow through. At first he was trying to act like he hadn't done anything and he was going to the trash can to put a bag in it. He kept saying, "Mom, I was going right now, I was doing it." Then after I didn't budge and told him he was done with his game and everything else in the house, his attitude got worse. He began acting as though he didn't care that he was on "Plan B". He said that it didn't matter because now he didn't have to do anything.

He was quite arrogant for a couple of days. It was a Wednesday when he was first placed on "Plan B". By Friday he was pretty bored and did a few chores to earn some money for some things. He was able to purchase rent of the trampoline for $5 for the month and he bought three pieces of paper and a pencil for 25 cents. He also rented a movie we had, with rent of the TV for one time to watch the movie, for a total of $2. He finally ran out of chores to do to earn money and he was bored out of his mind. He realized that the amount he could earn by doing the very simplistic chores within our home didn't even come close to paying for the amount of items that he had free access to on "Plan A".

By Sunday he had changed his tune and was much more humble. He was begging to be back on "Plan A". I made him finish out the week on "Plan B" to really instill the message I was trying to get across. It was a wonderful and powerful lesson for all the children. They all learned that I just wasn't asking that much of them for what they were getting in return.

We went for about a year with the impending threat of "Plan B". It worked well and the children were petrified of it. It worked great for getting chores done, however it still didn't solve the problem of teaching them to be respectful of each other and to not harass each other at every opportunity. I could not stand watching the children hurt each other emotionally and constantly pick on each other. I felt there had to be some serious consequences for doing so.

Remember that this was prior to Respect Rocks, so I was still trying anything I could think of. I decided that each time the kids were mean to each other, they would have to do something nice for the person they were mean to and the person they were mean to got to decide what they wanted. For example, they could get a back massage or have the person play a game with them or a foot massage or whatever. This worked for a while. One time my step-son Jack did something mean to Haedyn and she made him play Barbies with her which included Jack being one of the girl Barbies. That was funny. He was a very good sport about it but you could tell he didn't enjoy it at all and of course Haedyn loved every minute of it.

There was also a time that Connor owed Marissa. She made him give her a foot massage, which wasn't too bad except she made him use girly smelly floral lotion. The girly floral smell was difficult to get off his hands so Marissa loved that.

Although the kids had some fun with this plan and it lasted a while, it seemed to also promote bickering about who had started a fight or argument or who picked on whom first. They would each just end up owing each other something, which essentially cancelled each other's payments out. It began turning out that no one was paying up. It also seemed to give additional incentive to be mean to each other. If one child owed for being mean, it gave ammo to the person he/she owed to, and therefore that person often felt entitled to be mean back...because the person they were mean to owed them...right???!!! Confused yet??? Ya....you can see how this became just another cyclical damaging and ineffective pattern.

Writing about these things now makes me laugh. My family has come such a long way. Prior to Respect Rocks, I was just about at my wits end!

Chapter 6:

RESPECT ROCKS: The Competition

Now to get back to the exciting part! The
competition! During our first few competitions with
Respect Rocks, I realized that I was on to something. It
was simple and easy for the children to understand. The
reward or discipline was immediate as they watched their
own personal jars fill up or diminish based on their acts.
This was exactly what I wanted because I felt it was a
metaphor for their individual and personal growth.
Respect Rocks teaches them that everything they do
matters and, positive or negative, will directly impact them
personally.

On that note of "every point counts" is a lesson
that has been learned by my children several times. When
my step-children come to visit, we put the competition
between the children that are always in the home on hold
and have a separate competition while all of the children
are there. In one of the competitions that lasted two
weeks, the winner came down to one rock. Brielle had
gotten 123 rocks while Marissa had gotten 122. Marissa
was so frustrated. Although it was all in good spirit, she
kept thinking of all the simple things that she could have
done to earn that one rock. It was a good life lesson to
teach them all that every little thing matters. Even
something that doesn't seem like much can be the one
thing that puts you ahead or behind.

Connor also learned this. In one of the competitions, he lost by three rocks. During that competition, he had said that he had cleaned up his breakfast when he hadn't done it. He wasn't lying about it but I only award the rocks for meal clean-up if all facets of the clean-up are completed. For example you cannot earn the rocks for cleaning up your breakfast if you forgot to put the milk or cereal away. Even if you put your dish in the dishwasher, the task is not complete without putting away everything you got out to make your breakfast. Connor put his dishes away but forgot that he had left the cereal out. He then asked for his two rocks for the task but because he asked without actually completing the entire task, it cost him double of what he would have earned. Therefore, he lost four rocks. Those four rocks would have made him the winner considering in the end he had only lost the competition by three rocks.

Just as tasks and chores should be age appropriate, so is the earning of Respect Rocks. What I mean is, the more time consuming or difficult tasks are, the more rocks they are awarded. I contemplated this element of Respect Rocks for a while. At first I thought that I didn't want the younger kids to be discouraged because the older kids were earning more rocks for bigger tasks. But the long and the short of it is that they are older and should be earning more money. If I were giving an allowance, I would probably pay it based on chores completed. Since the older kids would most likely be doing the bigger tasks, they would be earning more money. So I felt that Respect

Rocks should be earned in a similar way. However, a younger child may earn more rocks than an older child would for doing the same task, especially one that may take more thought or effort for the younger child versus the older child. It really is task specific. I was a little concerned about how it would all play out and I didn't want any of the children to get discouraged and luckily, that is not what has happened.

The funny thing is that the first competition, was won by Jensen; the five year old!! He did great! Although the older kids were earning more rocks at a shot, the youngest one was doing the age appropriate simplistic things, earning every little rock he could. In the end, all those simplistic things put him ahead. He has actually won the competition more times than any other child. The system really does work for every age group and the younger ones can really hold their own.

Chapter 7:

Adjustment To The System: EVERYBODY EARNS SOMETHING

The first time all six children were in the competition together, was when I realized that having only one winner was somewhat discouraging to the others. As I said before, I originally liked the idea of one winner with a sort of winner takes all motto. Because the first competition with all six children together was only a two-week competition, the winner would get $20 versus the $50 that was the prize for winning the longer competitions. However a few days into this first competition with all six kids, I realized that I needed to make a few adjustments to my newfound plan.

In the beginning of the competition, the older girls were winning by a landslide and the competition was basically becoming between the two of them. Within the first few days the energy from the other kids was quickly dwindling as the older girls were obviously running away with the prize. I decided that to keep up energy and spirits of the entire team, we needed a second, third, fourth, fifth and sixth place prize as well. So I sat all 6 of them down and explained the change of rules. I told them that now the top winner would be getting $25 instead of $20. We would then have an additional 5 winners with the prizes being $20, $15, $10, $5 and $1 respectively. (As I said before, you can adjust this amount to anything within your means and budget).

The kids were thrilled and the energy in our home absolutely skyrocketed!! I have to say this was one of my favorite competitions! I don't think my house has ever been so clean and organized! To this day, whenever they are all here together, the competition is on! Jack and Brielle (my husband's children from California) always look forward to it when they come for an extended visitation and I love the energy it gives to our home!! It is so nice to see them creatively working so hard.

They clean out everything. The playroom, the garage, the linen closet, my closet, under the bathroom sinks, the pantry, the kitchen cabinets, the laundry room and cabinets, the TV cabinet, organizing games and movies, cleaning the windows, the doors, the baseboards, shower doors, vacuuming the couch and under the couch.....anything and everything they can think of to earn extra rocks. They do tasks individually and for bigger tasks, they work in groups. I have been amazed at what they come up with to earn rocks.

Two summers ago, we went up to my dad's condo in Pinetop. All six kids were with us and we were in the midst of a competition. My husband and I decided that since we were up there for five days, the competition would continue there as well. My grandparents also have a condo in the same complex. Not only were the kids continuing to help keep our condo clean and organized, they were branching out to help my grandparents as well. They helped them bring in firewood, they swept off the porches, and helped with other miscellaneous things that came up. It was wonderful! They were coming up with anything they could to earn Respect Rocks. It really made them aware of things that needed to be done and helped them branch out to help others. I was very proud of them.

Another time while we were at home in the midst of a competition, something quite funny happened. The kids were all working hard to earn rocks. One night at about 11pm, my husband and I had just fallen asleep in our room. Assuming that all the children were also snug in their beds, I got a call on my cell phone, which is always next to my bed. The call was from Marissa's cell phone. This was very odd to me because she and Brielle sleep in the room right next to ours so I couldn't figure out why on earth she would be calling us. Obviously curious and concerned, I answered the phone. Marissa was on the line almost hysterical. I told her she had to calm down so that I could understand what she was saying.

As it turns out, she and Brielle were hiding in the bathroom because they heard noises in the kitchen. As they continued to listen, the noises also continued. They knew the other kids were asleep in their beds and so were my husband and I. Their only conclusion was that someone had broken into the house and the uninvited guest was rummaging around in the kitchen. I told them to stay in the bathroom and my husband and I would check it out. On our way to the kitchen, I popped my head in the bathroom and Marissa and Brielle were both sitting on the bathroom sink absolutely terrified. We told them to stay there and my husband and I went cautiously into the kitchen. Much to our surprise we found the two oldest boys, Connor and Jack, cleaning out the kitchen cupboards after everyone else had gone to bed, in an attempt to have one up on the girls the next morning! Although we explained to the boys this shouldn't be done in the middle of the night, we commended them for their efforts. The girls were so embarrassed and went back to bed. The boys basked in their glory of earning more rocks and to this day, it continues to be a source of laughter and entertainment for our family.

All in all, making adjustments to the system and having everyone earn something did help in keeping everyone involved. The kids were so excited to do things. They worked together and were very creative in the way they did it. This was exactly what I was trying to accomplish with Respect Rocks. I really wanted to teach them to think for themselves. See something that needs to be done, and DO IT!

Chapter 8:

Loss of Gusto For the System

At one point, after about a year of following the system, the kids' excitement for Respect Rocks started to wear off. They got tired and were not trying as hard. They realized that as long as they had more rocks than the other kids, they would still win. This did not make me happy and was certainly not in line with my intention. They were slacking big time and were losing rocks left and right. I realized by looking at our jars, that there was a good chance that I had accumulated more rocks than any of them. Considering that I can only get rocks if they lose rocks, this was very disappointing to me.

So, I sat them down and told them that this particular competition was coming to an end soon. I relayed my disappointment and I informed them that if I ended up with more rocks than all of them individually, then they would all be on "Plan B". I told them that at least one of them had to earn more rocks than the number that had accumulated in my jar. If no one did, then they would all be on "Plan B". As I have stated before, my children are horrified by the idea of "Plan B" so this was a good wake up call for them.

After I spoke with them about it, they were off to the races, doing anything and everything they could to earn rocks. In the end Connor won with 152 rocks. I had 128, Marissa had 127, Haedyn had 82 and Jensen had 81.

Because Connor won and had more rocks than me, he received the $50. Because the other kids ended up with less rocks than me, they were each docked $5 from their respective reward amounts.

After that competition was over, the kids informed me that they were working together more than I knew at the time. Because they realized that Connor was the closest to catching up to me, they devised a plan to help him win as a way to save them all from "Plan B". They were going around the house finding things for him to do and having him tell them to put things away. Although it was obviously not my first choice to have this particular competition end that way, I was happy to see them working together. The kids know how important it is to me for them to work together, so they banked on me not being upset with them. I wasn't. They worked together and in the end, my point was well taken. They have never again allowed my jar, filled with the rocks they have lost, to surpass their jars, which are filled with the rocks they have earned. Once again, I have to give credit to "Plan B".

Another time, when we had all six kids together, they just weren't trying as hard as they originally were for prior competitions. They were not losing rocks, so my jar was not filling more than theirs, but they were not earning near as many rocks either. I had seen them in competitions before so I knew their potential. This time, they were only sticking with the basic tasks that were automatic rocks and not really doing anything to go above and beyond. Because of this, when this particular competition ended, I decreased the amount of money that each person received. They were not happy with that and they realized they had better step it up again. If they wanted the greater amount of money, they had to work for it. This has never again been a problem and the kids always earn the highest amount possible.

Gusto Returns and is Better Than Ever

In the Fall of 2010, the children were in a competition that lasted four months. There were three of them in the home at the time; Connor age twelve, Haedyn age nine, and Jensen age six. They were all working so hard and their cups of rocks were almost equal the entire competition. This made me very happy as they were all working so hard. We honestly could not tell by looking at the jars, which child would be the victorious winner of the top prize. I was so proud of the children. They all worked so hard and all three of them were very much engaged in the competition from the beginning to the end. When it came time to end the competition they were all within fifteen rocks of each other. My youngest child Jensen won the $50 followed by Haedyn and then Connor. Because they all worked so hard, I increased the second and third reward amounts. I thought this was fair since in other competitions, I had decreased it when I saw little effort. So this time, it was only fair to increase it when I saw such consistent positive effort.

Haedyn received $40 and Connor received $30. The children were thrilled. In the end, I figured it was over such a long period of time and they had all done so well that they deserved it. Additionally, had I been paying them allowance at say $5 per week per child, it would have totaled approximately $180. Therefore, I would have paid out well over the $120 it ended up costing me using the Respect Rocks system.

Christmas 2010 was shortly after that competition ended. As our big gift, we gave the entire family a cruise to the Mexican Riviera. We would be going a few months later in April. We told the kids in advance that there would be a lot of things on the ship they may want to buy as well as shops for souvenirs in Mexico. We advised them that they would need to use their own money. I cannot believe the competition that was created during that three and a half month period before the cruise. There were still only three children in this particular competition and I actually ran out of rocks!! When I first ran out, I physically took 50 rocks from each child's jar and just knew that I would add 50 back to their grand totals during the final tabulation. I then reused the rocks, to continue filling the jars as the children earned more. However, I quickly ran out of those rocks as well! I finally ended up keeping tabs of the additional earned rocks on a piece of paper. In the end, Connor had 548 rocks, Jensen came in second with 469 and Haedyn had 330! Wow....was I ever impressed! I again increased the amount of the respective prizes to

$50, $40 and $30. I again felt that the children worked very hard and very much earned it.

In a more recent competition, I offered another change to the plan and monies earned. As the competition was coming to a close, Jensen (age eight at the time) and Connor (age fourteen at the time) were in a close race. They had both filled more than one jar. In the final days of the competition, they were each doing anything and everything they could think of to earn rocks. My house was spotless and Jensen even alphabetically organized the shelf of DVDs! They both worked so hard that it was painful to think that only one of them was going to get the $50 top prize. Although second place won $25, I still felt bad because they were both working equally as hard.

So I offered a deal. On the day the competition ended, before we counted the rocks, I offered to increase the prize amount for the top two winners. Instead of being a combined $75 ($50 for first place and $25 for second place), I offered to up it to $80 and no matter who ended up with the most rocks, they would each win $40. The stipulation however, was that they both had to agree to the change, before the rocks were counted. If they didn't both agree, then the amounts of money won, would stand as originally established.

From simply looking at the jars, it was impossible to tell who had won. Jensen decided he didn't want to take the chance with loosing and only getting $25, so he was happy to agree to the change and getting $40. However after long contemplation, Connor decided that he was going to take the chance at the full $50. Since they didn't both agree to the change in earnings, the amounts stayed at $50 for the top winner and $25 for second place. I counted the rocks and before I told them their amounts, I asked them a final time if they were good with their previous decisions, giving Connor one last chance to make the change. He again confirmed that he wanted to go for the full $50. In the end, Connor had 364 and Jensen had 374, winning by only 10 rocks!! It was definitely a lesson in being stingy for Connor. I think Karma had a little something to do with that one!

Earning Rocks for Deeds Outside of Our Home & Family

I mentioned earlier that my kids also earn rocks for doing things outside of our home. These examples are probably some my favorites because they show that the children have learned to step outside of themselves and consider other people's needs.

We recently moved to California and we spend a lot of time at the beach. Often the kids will come out of the ocean carrying trash. They show me the trash and then they throw it away. If there is not a trash can at the beach, they will keep it in a sack and will throw it away when we get home. They always earn rocks for this. Jensen does it the most and he is always finding trash to throw away to help keep our earth clean.

Another example is something that happened at school with Haedyn. I didn't know about it until her teacher mentioned it at her parent/ teacher conference. The teacher said that there is a special needs child in Haedyn's class. She told me that Haedyn is always the first one to help the child out and that Haedyn goes out of her way to make sure the child feels included. At first the other children didn't really know how to respond to the special needs child. Haedyn on the other hand immediately jumped right in to help the boy whenever he needed. This is a perfect example of the purpose of Respect Rocks; seeing something that needs to be done and doing it. The teacher said that now, the other children have followed Haedyn's lead and often step in to help the young boy. The teacher got choked up as she told me about it and was so touched by Haedyn's example to the other children. I was of course beyond proud of Haedyn and quickly rewarded her with rocks when I returned home.

Connor has also earned rocks for mowing the neighbor's lawn. His lawn is connected to ours and instead of just mowing our side, Connor sometimes goes the extra mile and mows the neighbors lawn too.

Whether it is picking up trash at the beach or on the way home from school, helping another child out, mowing the neighbors lawn or helping them carry in groceries, my kids often find ways to help out other people. Respect Rocks has taught them to recognize when something needs to be done, and do it.

Chapter 9:

RESPECT ROCKS Encompasses Everything!!

RESPECT ROCKS: Treating Each Other with Kindness

In addition to earning rocks for doing tasks, chores or helping others, I utilize the system to tackle one of the biggest parenting problems of all: getting our children to be nice to each other! Impossible you say? It actually isn't with Respect Rocks. It is quite simple. The children can earn or lose rocks for having respect and being nice to each other. As I said earlier in the book, the kids lose rocks _to_ the person they were mean to. This is probably the most effective part of the plan because it is actually a difference of two rocks; it is one lost for them and one gained for the sibling. This has made a huge difference with the peace and continuity within our home.

For example, Haedyn, the youngest girl, is often the brunt of the jokes, pranks and personal attacks, mostly from the boys. I cannot even express what an improvement I have seen in this. Now that the boys actually lose rocks to Haedyn for being nasty to her, they really think twice before engaging in their antagonistic behavior towards her. Although they sometimes still mumble things under their breath or to each other, the direct attacks towards her have significantly decreased.

On one particular occasion when we first initiated the system, Haedyn was sitting on the couch playing with a wooden sword. Jack walked up to her and simply took the sword from her and walked away playing with the sword with a smile. This was a normal scenario for both of the older boys to act towards Haedyn. They were bigger so they knew they could. Plus, they loved the reaction that they would get from her, which with Haedyn is just short of complete hysteria. This particular time, I was right there and saw the whole thing. Haedyn initially started to freak but then she remembered our Respect Rocks system. She just looked at me and said "Mom!" I simply said to Jack, "Now you have to give her a rock." Haedyn smiled of course and although Jack didn't like the idea, he smiled too, knowing that he had broken the rules that were very clear.

I then asked Jack after I got the smile of acknowledgement from him, "So was taking that sword worth it?" He smiled, shook his head, and said "No". It was a lesson well learned and I was thrilled because I didn't have to yell or even get mad. Additionally, a situation that would have normally created drama, hysteria, tears and crisis in our home, instead created harmony, peace and an impact for the future. To this day, Jack has never done anything like that again.

Connor is a little more tempted as he and Haedyn live together full-time and have more opportunity for interaction. But Haedyn is growing older now and is occasionally the instigator herself. Connor will of course tell you it is always her but either way, they both are forced to take responsibility for their negative actions towards each other. Jensen, the youngest child just under Haedyn, has also learned how to antagonize her. But again, Haedyn isn't totally innocent so they often lose rocks to me for their joint attacks on each other. Although kids will be kids and the idea of perfect constant harmony is a dream far off, Respect Rocks creates the avenue of responsibility for them and a source of decreased yelling and increased peace for me.

RESPECT ROCKS: Positive Attitude

I also have explained to the children that attitude is so important. There will always be things that they do not like to do. This will unfortunately happen throughout their entire lives in everything; school, work, athletics, home, finances.....everywhere. I teach that although we do not always have choices about what we have to do, we do have a choice of how we handle those things. I am teaching them that understanding this is an essential part of their future. So I also utilize the Respect Rocks system to instill this concept in them. They have often lost rocks just for how they respond to me after I ask them to do something. Although they still get up and complete the task, if they have a poor attitude filled with sighs, anger, negativity and complaints, they will lose a rock instead of earn one for the task. They have all learned quickly that attitude is where the majority of the effort resides. I am very intolerant of poor attitudes as this is where there is always a choice to be made.

RESPECT ROCKS: Homework Completion and Grades

The system can also be used to encourage homework completion. The children can earn a rock for doing their homework on their own without being asked. In turn, they will lose a rock if they disregard their homework or forget to do it. They also lose a rock if they remember but are racing to finish it just as they are supposed to be going to bed or worse, right before school. They have learned that homework is their responsibility to complete and not mine to remind them.

On this note, I provide another opportunity to earn rocks for grades. The children earn four rocks per "A" and three rocks per "B". I do not give rocks for less than a "B" because I feel that is just average effort. However if there ever came a time that one of my children were to earn a "C" but I felt they had applied themselves and done what they could, I would certainly award them with rocks for effort.

Connor has made an unbelievable turn around when it comes to completing homework, getting good grades and taking a personal role in his own education. He is now excited about getting good grades and realizes that it is his responsibility. Prior to the Respect Rocks system, I was concerned that he would be a slacker the rest of his life, always trying to get out of work. Needless to say, his work ethic was significantly lacking. I cannot believe the 180-degree turn around that he made in the first year of starting Respect Rocks. He has learned honor and respect for himself and his responsibilities. He completes his homework without being asked, he gets his projects done well in advance of their due dates and is always checking his grades online. He used to be a "B , C" and sometimes "D" student. Now he gets mostly all "A's" with an occasional "B".

Remember, Connor is also the child who had to actually test out "Plan B". In addition to becoming an almost straight "A" student, he is always the first child to jump up and get his Saturday chores done quickly. He knows to do them right the first time because he realizes that if he doesn't, I will make him do it again. He has additionally learned that sitting around whining and complaining about it gets you nowhere and is simply a waste of time. He knows now that it is just best to get it done and move on with your day. He has learned the avenue to more play time/ video game time is getting your work done first. Work Hard *then* Play Hard. This positive change in Connor as well as all the children is incredible and is largely due to the Respect Rock system. Respect Rocks really is a fun, competitive and effective way for the children to learn to take responsibility for their own actions and individual outcomes. Connor is a perfect example of this life altering success.

Chapter 10:

CONCLUSION

All in all, Respect Rocks has made a profound difference in our home. So much, that I felt the need to share the system with others. Although it is unlikely to create *perfect* harmony between siblings, especially at this young age, this system has created a sense of harmony and continuity within our home that nothing else has ever been able to provide. My children are excited about it and actually enjoy it. It has become such an intricate part of our home and is truly creating responsible children. I am frequently faced with a frustrated parent through friends and work who describe the source of their frustration as their unruly children. I continually think to myself, Respect Rocks could fix that!

After over 3 years of following the program, I can honestly say that nothing has ever come as close to creating consistency and positive discipline within our home and family, as Respect Rocks has. It is a system that has lasted because it can so easily be adjusted to fit the multiple levels of ever changing circumstances that life offers.

My kids and I also have the best relationship we have ever had. There is a mutual respect and understanding of what is acceptable and what is not. I have often heard stories of parents who have horrible relationships with their kids. When delving deeper into the specifics of those poor relationships, it is not always the kids who are to blame. Our children learn by example and if we are not extending respect to them, how can they ever learn how to truly be respectful to us? Showing respect towards our children is the first critical step in teaching them to become respectful towards others. If you opt to instead, simply create fear in your children, it will not last forever. Trust me, fear passes in the teenage years, and you are often left with a rebellious teenager. On the other hand, if you start teaching personal responsibility and mutual respect from a young age, you are bound to end up with a much better outcome. My kids are not afraid of me at all. However, they never want to disappoint me, as I never want to disappoint them. It is a two way street of value, expectations and reliability. Simply put, it is RESPECT.

We are currently in the midst of a newly started competition. The energy is so high and the competition is tight. They are having fun and their attitudes are top notch. They have learned to be thankful and appreciative for all that they are given and are also able to recognize the needs of others. Not only are they able to recognize those needs but they are learning to act on them. They have also learned that attitude is 90% of the battle. For the most part when I ask them to do something, I am greeted with a "Yes mother whom I love so much, I would love to do that for you." It is obviously mildly sarcastic, but they clearly get the point.

If it sounds too good to be true, I challenge you to try it for yourself and your family. I am sure you will need to add your personal touch to your own system and possibly tweak it to fit your own familial needs. But if you stick with it, I believe you will have similar results. That is unless you are one of the few families whose children are perfect and sit around every night singing *Kumbuya* together. However, if you were one of these people, my guess is that you would not be reading this book. So you owe it to yourself and your family to implement a behavior and incentive program that will create an amazing and profound energy in your home. This positive energy cycle will instill instincts in your children that will stay with them forever and that (without sounding too cliché) is PRICELESS!!

I additionally extend my personal positive energy and thoughts your way and wish you well in your endeavors as you create and implement this new system. I sincerely hope that it makes as much of a profound difference in your home, as it has in mine!! Best Wishes!!

RESPECT ROCKS

The What To Do, When To Do and How To Do It Manual

(Generic version)

Modify and customize this manual to fit your family's specific needs. Either fill in the blanks that I have provided or simply use it as a template to create your own Manual.

BEDROOMS

Daily

1. Bed made.
2. Dirty clothes put in hamper or _____.
3. Water cups, from night before, taken to kitchen sink/ dishwasher before getting a new one.
4. Nothing left on floors.
5. Picked up prior to going to bed and prior to going to school.

_____

_____

_____

_____

Weekly done on: _____

6. #1, 2, 3, 4 & 5 from above.
7. Closet cleaned out, shoes organized.
8. Dresser cleaned off AND organized.
9. Dust/ wipe down.
10. Garbage that has collected ANYWHERE in room be thrown away.

_____

_____

_____

_____

BEDTIME/ BATHTIME RITUAL

1. Bedtime on school nights is _____ SHARP! Bedtime on weekends is _____ SHARP. Bedtime means in bed with lights off. Homework complete and bedtime rituals already complete. Such as, already gone to the bathroom, already have drinks and already told mom & dad whatever it is you need to tell them.
2. Prior to going to bed, the family room, bedrooms and _____ must be picked up.
3. For every minute past _____, double the time will be deducted from bedtime the following night.
4. If you are unable to get up in the morning when you are told, bedtime will be changed to an earlier time.
5. Showers, baths or whatever you need to do to get cleaned up, changed and ready for bed is to be started at _____. (Unless we are not home yet)
   a. After shower/bath/changing clothes etc, ALL CLOTHES, SHOES, HAIR TIES, OR ANYTHING ELSE THAT WAS BROUGHT/ PUT INTO THE BATHROOM AS A RESULT OF THE BEDTIME RITUAL, SHALL BE PICKED UP AND PUT IN THE APPROPRIATE PLACE!!!!!! NO EXCEPTIONS!!!!
   b. Brush and floss teeth. Use mouthwash. Put everything back after you are done!
6. If you are able to get all of the above bedtime requirements completed prior to bedtime, you are free to spend the left over time until bedtime as you choose.
7. If you are successful with bedtime throughout the week, a late night can be earned for the weekend.

_____

_____

_____

_____

CLEANING THE BATHROOMS

FULL CLEANING

1. Remove items from counter.
2. Use _____ cleaner on counters, sink and faucet. Use small to moderate amount on counters. Using a wet washcloth and a circular motion, buff cleaner onto counters, sink AND drain, removing dirt and grime.
3. Rinse washcloth with water and wipe wet washcloth on counter and sinks.
4. Repeat step 3 until cleaner is removed.
5. Dry sink and countertops with dry towel.
6. Clean mirrors with glass cleaner and paper towels. Repeat until ALL streaks and spots are off mirror.
7. Step back and look at mirror from ALL angles to assure that ALL spots and streaks have been removed.
8. Repeat step 7, because there is a good chance there are still spots and streaks.
9. Put toilet cleaner in toilet. Let sit while cleaning ENTIRE toilet with antibacterial wipes or antibacterial cleaner and paper towels. Use one wipe for outer toilet (everything but seat), and one wipe to clean the top of the seat and THEN under seat...in that order.
10. Use _____ to wipe down counter items and place them NICELY and ORDERLY on counter.

_____
_____
_____
_____
_____
_____
_____

PARTIAL BATHROOM CLEANING

1. Using antibacterial wipes, wipe down counter, faucet, sink and drain.
2. Toilet may also need a wipe down with antibacterial wipes. Do this as needed. (If you think there is any chance that mom/ dad will think it is needed, then it is.)

_____

_____

_____

_____

***Full cleaning to be done every _____ by ALL children.

***Partial cleaning to be done on the following days by:

Monday: _____

Tuesday: _____

Wednesday: _____

Thursday: _____

VACUUMING/ CLEANING THE FLOORS

1. Carpets should be vacuumed as follows:

_____

_____

_____

2. Tile should be vacuumed or swept as follows:

_____

_____

_____

3. Wood floors should be cleaned as follows:

_____

_____

_____

4. A systematic approach should be done while vacuuming to assure that all areas are covered. This is more difficult to tell on the tile or wood floors. Thus a systematic approach of "tile by tile" or "line by line" aids in this process. This is also helpful when vacuuming the carpet as you will see the lines where you have and have not vacuumed.
5. If the vacuum will not get something, especially along the baseboards, detach the suction hose and vacuum along the baseboard.
6. ALL kitchen chairs and barstools should be moved and area under table and bar vacuumed.
7. If there is something in the way or on the floor that is inhibiting you from vacuuming, move it and/or put it away and proceed with vacuuming. Do NOT just leave the item there and vacuum around it.
8. MOPPING IS DONE AS FOLLOWS:

_____

_____

_____

_____

CAR

1. If you bring it into the car it is your responsibility to get it out.
2. If you fail to get any item that you brought into the car, out of the car, you will no longer be able to bring items into the car and this may result in losing that item.
3. Garbage needs to be picked up daily. This includes wrappers, cups, drinks etc.
4. Car is to be cleaned on _____. This includes vacuuming and wiping down the inside. Washing the outside.
5. If it becomes a problem for anyone to leave items in the car, trash in the car or disrespecting the car, that person will loose the FREE privilege of getting rides in the car and will be charged an appropriate fee for receiving rides in the car, to and from their activities.

_____
_____
_____
_____

HOMEWORK

1. Homework shall be started at _____ sharp.
2. If you have _____ or any other conflicting afternoon activity, then homework shall be started at _____, or immediately after returning from the activity.
3. You are welcome to start homework earlier if preferred.
4. If we are not home at the above stated times, homework shall be started immediately upon arrival home or can be done in the car.
5. Homework shall be completed before playing outside, watching TV, playing video games, or doing any other free-time activities.
6. YOUR homework is YOUR responsibility.
7. It is not mom or dad's responsibility to hound you, nag you, or remind you of your homework.

_____
_____
_____
_____

LAUNDRY

1. Separate laundry baskets will be provided for each child. Your basket is your responsibility. Put away all clothes in baskets. Older children help the younger children. Specifically, _____ help _____, _____ help _____ and _____ help _____.
2. Clothes should be folded and put away in the appropriate places. NOT just shoved in the drawers.
3. Hang shirts and other hanging items on appropriate hangers AND hang up in closets.
4. Socks should be folded and put away.
5. Remaining hangers should be hung back up or put in their appropriate place.
6. Pick up lint, wrappers and other laundry trash and put in garbage.
7. Put used dryer sheets in garbage.
8. Laundry NOT complete until all remnants of laundry is put in its appropriate place.

_____
_____
_____
_____

***Laundry is done on _____ and whenever else Mom/ Dad says.

SET-UP & CLEAN-UP OF DINNER/ MEAL DISHES

Before dinner

1. Set table with napkin, fork, and drink for each person. Add spoon and knife if needed.
2. Make sure table is clean prior to setting. If it is not clean, wipe it off well with kitchen washcloth or sponge. Use antibacterial cleaner if needed. Remember, you will be eating off this table. Germs left on table will end up in your mouth when you eat.

_____

_____

_____

_____

After dinner

1. Clean off dishes in sink with water and sponge and place in orderly fashion in dishwasher.

2. If unable to put in dishwasher, large pots and pans should be cleaned WELL with soap and water. With the exception of all STONE-ware or _____. These items must be done by hand, not put in dishwasher and cleaned in the following manner.

_____

_____

These items are the responsibility of _____.

3. Dry the dishes from step #2 with a fresh, CLEAN towel.

4. Once all possible dishes are placed in dishwasher, do the following to start the dishwasher. _____

_____

_____

_____

_____

5. Wipe off countertops with wet washcloth/ sponge until clean. Wipe down with kitchen antibacterial cleaner and paper towels or antibacterial wipes.

_____

_____

_____

_____

***All above listed tasks should be done by all available children, working together as a team or on the following individualized schedule. (assign a person for each day)

_____

_____

_____

Individual meals/ snacks

1. Anything that you got out to make or prepare your meal or snack must be put away. This includes the cereal box, milk, utensils, wrappers, cans, containers, ANYTHING. If you got it out, then it is your responsibility to put it away.

2. Wash and put away your dishes.

3. Wipe off the counter or table.

TAKING OUT THE TRASH

1. Remove the trash bag from the trashcan. Collect all trash that is surrounding the trashcan that has somehow not managed to make it into the actual trashcan.
2. Be sure to collect trash from ALL cans including but not limited to: the kitchen, bathrooms, bedrooms, kids rooms, parent's room and _____.
3. Make sure all trash is removed from the bottom of the can and be sure that can is empty. (Even if it means using your hands to remove the trash from the bottom of the can.)
4. A new garbage bag should be placed in ALL the cans. Use _____ bags for the following trashcans: _____. The smaller trashcans require a _____ as a trash liner.
5. Once all trash is collected, take it outside to the large garbage can outside. DO NOT PUT IT ON THE SIDE OF THE LARGE OURSIDE TRASH CAN!! Actually put it IN the large outside trashcan.
6. WASH YOUR HANDS.....WITH SOAP!

_____
_____
_____
_____

*** Kitchen trash should be taken out daily and other cans should be taken out weekly <u>at minimum</u>. Weekly trash emptying will be done on _____.

***All trash may need to be taken out more frequently than previously mentioned and should be checked DAILY and taken out as needed.

***If it is full and/or overflowing, take it out using the above mentioned process.

***Even if you think it is not full and overflowing, there is a good chance it is.......so empty it anyways.

GENERAL FAMILY RULES

1. If you get it out, put it back and/ or clean it up.
2. If you break it, fix it or you are responsible for replacing it.
3. Clean up after yourself. NO one here is hired as your personal maid.
4. Do what Mom or Dad ask the first time. You have ears. Use them to listen the first time.
5. Be kind to each other.
6. Name calling and hitting or pushing will NOT be tolerated.

_____

_____

_____

_____

_____

_____

_____

_____

_____
(TASK)

(STEPS)

1. _____

2. _____

3. _____

4. _____

5. _____

6. _____

7. _____

8. _____

9. _____

10. _____

11. _____

12. _____

13. _____

14. _____

15. _____

_____
(TASK)

(STEPS)

1. _____

2. _____

3. _____

4. _____

5. _____

6. _____

7. _____

8. _____

9. _____

10. _____

11. _____

12. _____

13. _____

14. _____

15. _____

_____
(TASK)

(STEPS)

1. _____

2. _____

3. _____

4. _____

5. _____

6. _____

7. _____

8. _____

9. _____

10. _____

11. _____

12. _____

13. _____

14. _____

15. _____

(TASK)

(STEPS)

1. _____

2. _____

3. _____

4. _____

5. _____

6. _____

7. _____

8. _____

9. _____

10. _____

11. _____

12. _____

13. _____

14. _____

15. _____

_____
(TASK)

(STEPS)

1. _____

2. _____

3. _____

4. _____

5. _____

6. _____

7. _____

8. _____

9. _____

10. _____

11. _____

12. _____

13. _____

14. _____

15. _____

_____

(TASK)

(STEPS)

1. _____

2. _____

3. _____

4. _____

5. _____

6. _____

7. _____

8. _____

9. _____

10. _____

11. _____

12. _____

13. _____

14. _____

15. _____

Made in the USA
Columbia, SC
31 January 2021